Bats

A Fun and Educational Book for Kids with Amazing Facts and Pictures

Table of Contents

Table of Contents.. 3

Introduction.. 5

Scientific Name 8

Appearance..10

Geography 13

Behavior 15

Reproduction 18

Social Life 21

Habitat 24

Senses 27

Feeding..30

Diet 33

Babies 36

Predators 39

Evolution 42

Population 45

Conservation Status 48

Health...51

Lifespan 54

Conclusion 57

Introduction

There are many different types of mammals in the order Chiroptera, including bats. They are the only mammals that can fly for extended periods of time, and they can be found anywhere on Earth outside the polar areas. More than 1,400 different species of bats have been identified, accounting for 20% of all known mammal species.

Bats occur in a wide range of sizes and shapes, with some species having wingspan lengths of more than 5 feet and others barely a few inches. These are nocturnal animals, and many of them rely on echolocation to find food in the shadows. Bats consume a range of foods, such as insects, fruit, nectar, and, in the case of vampire bats, even blood.

In many habitats, bats serve a vital ecological role. They are important plant pollinators and aid in the management of insect populations. Also, several types of bats are employed in scientific studies on the results of aging and ailments including cancer.

Despite playing crucial ecological and scientific roles, humans frequently have the wrong idea about and are afraid of bats. Many kinds of bats are harmless to people, although some are incorrectly thought to be hazardous. Yet, it's crucial to use caution while interacting with bats because some species can spread diseases like rabies.

Scientific Name

Chiroptera is the scientific term for bats, which in Greek means "hand-wing." Its name alludes to the fact that a bat can fly thanks to the development of extended fingers wrapped in a thin skin membrane. Megachiroptera, commonly referred to as fruit bats or flying foxes, and Microchiroptera are two suborders of the order Chiroptera (also known as echolocating bats).

The senses of smell and vision in bats are exceptional.

The smallest bat, the bumblebee, is barely 1.5 inches long and weighs less than a penny. The largest bat, the flying fox, can have a wingspan of more than 5 feet. Depending on the species, their fur may be brown, black, gray, or even vividly colored. Overall, bats have an interesting and distinctive appearance that is ideal for their life in the air.

Geography

The polar areas are the only places where bats cannot be found. They have colonized a wide variety of habitats, from woods and deserts to cities, thanks to their great adaptability. Several bat species migrate and cover great distances every year in search of food and mating places.

The tropics, particularly in South America and Southeast Asia, are where you can find the widest variety of bat species. In these areas, bats are crucial for seed dispersal and plant pollination. Although they hibernate in order to preserve energy during the winter, bats may also be found in temperate areas like North America and Europe.

Generally, bats are a very successful group of animals that have survived in a wide range of global conditions. They have been able to colonize a wide range of habitats and contribute significantly to many ecosystems thanks to their ability to fly and their capacity to adapt to a number of food sources.

Behavior

Based on their species and environment, bats display a variety of behaviors. The following are some typical traits of bat behavior:

Most bats are nocturnal, which means they spend the day sleeping and being active at night. With the aid of their extraordinarily keen hearing and echolocation, they can travel and find prey in the dark.

Social: Many different kinds of bats are social animals that frequently have colonies of thousands or even millions. These colonies may consist of one species or a number of species coexisting.

Bats roost in many different places, such as caves, trees, and buildings. They frequently snuggle together for warmth and may utilize the same roosting location for years.

Foraging: Bats consume a range of foods, such as insects, fruit, nectar, and, in the case of vampire bats, even blood.

Certain bat species are significant pollinators, while others aid in the management of insect populations.

Most bats mate in the fall and have one or two offspring in the spring. Born alive, young bats are fed by their mothers until they can fly and hunt for food on their own.

Hibernation: To conserve energy during the colder months, several species of bats hibernate in colder locations. To save energy, they may spend the night in caves or other protected areas and lower their body temperature and metabolic rate.

Overall, bats are fascinating animals that display a variety of activities and are crucial to many ecosystems. Because to their remarkable adaptability, they have flourished in a variety of global habitats.

Reproduction

Many species of bats have distinct reproductive strategies. The following are some general traits of bat reproduction:

The majority of bat species mate in the fall, and at this time, males frequently fight for the attention of females. While some species mate with just one partner, others engage in many partners' mating.

Delayed fertilization is a special reproductive trait that only female bats possess. The female is able to postpone fertilization after mating until the environment is suitable for childbirth and parenting.

Birth and gestation: The gestation period for the majority of bat species is only 4 to 6 weeks long. One or two pups are often born at a time, survive, and able to cling to their moms within hours of birth in the majority of bats. Until the young bats are old enough to fly and find food on their own, female bats nurse them with milk.

Female bats are very maternal and frequently establish nursing colonies where they share parental duties with other females. While scavenging for food, certain bat species may carry their young with them.

Longevity: In comparison to other mammals their size, bats live relatively lengthy lives. Several species have a wild life span of more than 20 years.

Overall, the reproduction process of bats is intricate and fascinating and has evolved to meet the particular requirements of their airborne lifestyle. Bats have developed a variety of techniques, such as delayed fertilization and intensive maternal care, to guarantee the survival of their offspring.

Social Life

Many social behaviors are displayed by bats, depending on their species and location. The following are some general traits of bat social behavior:

Numerous species of bats live in sizable colonies that might number in the tens of thousands or even millions. These colonies may consist of one species or a number of species coexisting. Even now, some bats exhibit cooperative behavior and share roosts.

Bats interact with one another by using a range of vocalizations, including echolocation. To communicate with other bats, they may also employ visual clues like body language or facial expressions.

Bats groom themselves extensively to keep their fur and wings clean and clear of parasites. They might groom themselves or other colony members.

Cooperation: Several species of bats cooperate with one

another by sharing food or cuddling together for warmth. Also, certain animals may cooperate to protect their colony from predators.

Bats may engage in a variety of mating activities, ranging from lifelong pair bonds to several mating partners. Other behaviors among some animals include courting displays and competition for mated partners.

Parenting: Female bats are extremely maternal and frequently establish nursing colonies where they cooperate in the upbringing of their young. While scavenging for food, some bat species will also bring their young with them.

Generally, bats engage in a variety of social activities and are able to engage in sophisticated social relationships. They are extremely gregarious creatures that frequently coexist in sizable colonies and exhibit a range of cooperative activities.

Habitat

Across the world, bats can be found in a variety of habitats, such as wetlands, grasslands, deserts, and forests. Following are a few typical attributes of bat habitats:

Many different species of bats have their roosts in caves or other underground locations, such as tunnels or abandoned mines. These roosts offer stability in temperature and safety from predators.

Trees and other vegetation: Some bat species roost in trees or other vegetation, grabbing hold of leaves or branches with their razor-sharp claws. These roosts can give birds access to food sources like fruit or insects.

Buildings in urban areas: Some bat species have adapted to city life and will spend the night in buildings or other structures, like tunnels or bridges. These roosts can give access to food supplies and protection from scavengers.

Water sources: Several bat species, like the fishing bat, roost close to bodies of water where they consume fish and other aquatic life.

Tropical rainforests: A variety of bat species, many of which play a vital role in pollination and seed dispersal, can be found in tropical rainforests.

Bats are generally very versatile and can be found in a variety of settings all over the world. They are vital components of numerous ecosystems and are crucial for pollination, seed dissemination, and pest management. But, habitat loss and other human activities are putting many bat populations in danger, so it's critical to safeguard their habitats and maintain their numbers.

Senses

In order to live an aerial lifestyle, bats have developed a specific set of senses. The following are some general traits of bat senses:

Bats fly in the dark using echolocation to find their way and find prey. They make loud noises and then keep an ear out for echoes that are reflected back from adjacent objects. As a result, they can visualize their surroundings and recognize objects in their path.

Although echolocation is the primary method of navigation for bats in the dark, they also have well-developed vision that enables them to perceive in dimly lit environments. Several bat species can also detect ultraviolet light, which facilitates their ability to find flowers and other food sources.

Smell: Bats utilize their keen sense of smell to locate food and locate the places where they sleep.

Touch: Bats can sense changes in air pressure and navigate

through challenging surroundings because to extraordinarily sensitive touch sensors in their wings. During grooming rituals, for example, they communicate with other bats by using their sense of touch.

In general, bats have a special set of senses that have evolved to fit their life in the air. For bats, echolocation is a particularly crucial sense since it enables them to move about and find prey in total darkness. Their other senses, including vision, smell, and touch, are also crucial to their survival and interpersonal relationships.

Feeding

The dietary habits of bats are highly varied, with several species specializing in various kinds of food. The following are some general traits of bat feeding:

Several bat species are insectivores, meaning they consume a variety of insects like moths, beetles, and mosquitoes. They can eat a lot of insects in one night and utilize echolocation to find their meal.

Fruit: Certain bat species are frugivores, relying mostly on fruit and nectar for food. For many plant species, they are crucial for pollination and seed dispersion.

Blood: Only three species of bats, all of which are found in Latin America, are known to only consume blood. These vampire bats make tiny punctures in other animals, usually livestock, and slurp on the blood using their tongues.

Fish: A few bat species, like the fishing bat, are piscivores, meaning they eat fish and other aquatic creatures.

Other: Several bat species consume a variety of things, including fruit, insects, and small vertebrates like frogs and lizards.

Overall, the dietary patterns of bats are highly varied, and they are significant members of many ecosystems. For many plant species, they are crucial seed dispersers and pollinators, and they also aid in the management of insect populations. Unfortunately, several bat species are in danger due to habitat loss and other human activities, which may negatively affect their feeding behaviors and chances of surviving.

Diet

Many kinds of bats consume a variety of foods, including insects, fruit, nectar, pollen, fish, and even blood. Further information on the various bat diets is provided below:

Bats that eat largely on insects like moths, beetles, and mosquitoes are known as insectivorous bats. These bats can eat a lot of insects in a single night and utilize echolocation to find their meal in the dark. It can be advantageous for the environment and the economy for insectivorous bats to manage insect populations.

Bats that are primarily fruit, nectar, and pollen eaters are known as frugivorous bats. These bats contribute to the maintenance of thriving ecosystems as they are significant seed dispersers and pollinators for many plant species. Certain frugivorous bat species may consume both insects and fruit.

Bat species that consume tiny vertebrates including frogs, lizards, and other bats are known as carnivorous bats. It is known that several carnivorous bat species, like the ghost bat and the fake vampire bat, eat other bats.

Piscivorous bats: Certain bats consume fish as well as other aquatic creatures including insects and crabs. Around water sources like rivers, lakes, and ponds, these bats can be found.

Only three species of bats, all of which can be found in Latin America, are known to be hematophagous. These vampire bats make tiny bites in other animals' flesh with their fangs and slurp up the blood with their tongues, usually livestock or birds.

Overall, bats eat a variety of foods and are vital pollinators, seed dispersers, pest controllers, and predators in many habitats. However because of the potential threat posed by habitat loss, climate change, and other human activities, it is critical to save bat habitats and maintain their populations.

Babies

The reproductive technique used by bats is distinctive and varies based on the species. The following are some general traits of bat babies:

Birth: The majority of bat species only have one young per year, while some larger species have triplets or even triplets. Species-specific birth dates range, but most bats give birth in the spring or summer after a few weeks to many months of gestation.

Bat pups are born naked, blind, and defenseless, and they are completely dependent on their mothers for both food and protection. Nonetheless, they grow quickly and, depending on the species, can be fully grown and independent in a matter of weeks to months.

Breast milk is produced by bat moms for their young, who are fed through their nipples. To aid in the puppies' rapid growth, the milk contains a lot of fat and protein.

Roosting: To nurture their young, bat moms frequently roost in enormous groupings known as maternity colonies. Depending on the species, there may be thousands of these colonies.

Weaning: When bat pups are completely grown and able to fly on their own, they are weaned from their mother's milk and start eating solid food.

Overall, bat infants are born small and defenseless, but they grow quickly and can quickly achieve complete independence. In what are known as maternity colonies, bat moms frequently gather in huge groupings to care for and defend their young. Understanding the distinct reproductive behaviors of each species of bat is crucial for their conservation and management because the time and duration of the reproductive cycle might differ by species.

Predators

The number of natural predators for bats varies by species and region, as does the degree of predation. Here are a few typical bat predators:

Birds of prey: Various bird species, including owls, hawks, and eagles, have been observed to feed on bats. These birds have the ability to capture bats in flight or remove them from roosts.

Rat snakes and coral snakes are two snake species that are known to prey on bats. In order to access bat roosts and capture flying bats, these snakes may scale trees and other structures.

Mammals: A number of animal species, including raccoons, weasels, and house cats, have been observed to hunt on bats. To access bat roosts and catch bats in flight, these mammals may scale trees and other constructions.

People: Humans can potentially pose a hazard to bats by

engaging in behaviors including habitat damage, roost site disruption, and purposeful bat slaughter motivated by ignorance or fear.

Generally, predation occurs naturally in the ecosystem, and bats have evolved a number of defense mechanisms to fend off or outsmart their predators, including irregular flight and roosting in inhospitable places. But since human activity can be a serious threat to bat populations, it's critical to safeguard their habitats and maintain their numbers.

Evolution

Scientists continue to study and argue over the evolution of bats since they are the only mammals that can fly. These are some important details regarding bat evolution:

Fossil evidence: The Eocene epoch, almost 50 million years ago, is when the oldest fossilized bats were discovered. These early bats may have been able to glide but not actually fly due to their short wings.

Evolution of flight: Although the evolution of flight in bats is still not fully understood, it is believed to have involved a number of adaptations, such as alterations to the hands and forelimbs, the creation of a light but sturdy skeletal system, and modifications to the muscle structure and metabolism.

Bats have evolved into more than 1,400 different species, accounting for about 20% of all mammal species. The adaption to various habitats, food supplies, and social systems have all contributed to this variety.

Relationships with other mammals: Although there is some disagreement on the precise relationships between bats and other mammals, it is generally accepted that bats are related to primates and tree shrews. Moreover, some scientists have hypothesized that bats might be more closely linked to insectivores or carnivores.

Ultimately, research into the evolution of bats is complicated and continuing, and much more has to be discovered about the development of flight in these extraordinary creatures. Nonetheless, due to their diversity and flexibility, bats are an important component of many ecosystems around the world and a fascinating subject for biologists.

Population

The number of bats varies depending on the species and region, but many bat populations worldwide are under threat from factors like habitat loss, disease, and climate change. These are some important details regarding bat populations:

The size of the bat population varies substantially depending on the species and the area. While some species of bat are common and have vast populations, others are rare or endangered.

Threats: Bat populations are threatened by a number of factors, such as disease, habitat loss and degradation, climate change, and human persecution.

White-nose sickness: A illness known as white-nose syndrome has killed millions of bats in North America, making it one of the biggest threats to bat populations in recent years. The sickness is brought on by a fungus that develops on the cheeks and wings of bats that are hibernating. This fungus causes the bats to wake up excessively and burn up their fat reserves, which results in famine and death.

Initiatives to protect and conserve bat populations worldwide include habitat restoration, disease control, and public awareness campaigns. Conservation organizations and government organizations are also involved in these efforts.

The population of bats is diverse and complex overall, with numerous species confronting a wide range of dangers. For bats to continue to play their crucial roles in ecosystems all around the world and for populations to be healthy and sustainable, conservation efforts are vital.

Conservation Status

Many bat species have different conservation statuses, but many of them are under peril and are considered vulnerable, endangered, or critically endangered. The following are some important details regarding bat conservation:

The IUCN, or International Union for the Conservation of Nature, The IUCN, which oversees a Red List of Endangered Species that contains several bat species, is the foremost authority on the conservation status of species. Out of the more than 1,400 bat species that are known, 246 are categorized as vulnerable, endangered, or severely endangered as of 2023.

Threats: Disease, climate change, habitat loss and degradation, and human persecution are the greatest risks to bat populations. Moreover, pesticides and other toxins, collisions with wind turbines and other structures, and disturbance of roost locations can all have a negative influence on bats.

Initiatives to protect and conserve bat populations worldwide include habitat restoration, disease control, and public awareness campaigns. Conservation organizations and government organizations are also involved in these efforts. Protecting and managing bat roost places, such as caves, mines, and other buildings where they congregate, is one of the most efficient ways to conserve bats.

Bats are very important to many ecosystems across the world because they help with pollination, seed dissemination, and insect control. The existence of these unusual and interesting creatures, as well as the health and sustainability of several ecosystems, depends on protecting bat populations.

Overall, the conservation status of bats varies depending on the species and region, but many bat populations are threatened and need protection in order to survive. Maintaining the variety and health of many ecosystems across the world requires protecting bat populations.

Health

Many diseases that can spread to humans and other animals are carried by bats. It's crucial to remember that the majority of bats do not transmit illness and do not directly endanger human health. The following are some important details regarding bat health:

Rabies, hantavirus, and coronaviruses like SARS-CoV-2 are a few diseases that can be spread to people by bats. It's crucial to remember that these diseases are only rarely transmitted to humans, and the majority of human cases result from close contact with diseased bats.

The immune systems of bats make them the only mammals capable of surviving and even thriving in the presence of a wide variety of viruses and other diseases. To better understand how the immune system of bats functions and to create new drugs and vaccines for human diseases, researchers are examining bat immune systems.

White-nose syndrome: In recent years, one of the biggest

health risks to bat populations has been the condition known as "white-nose syndrome," which is brought on by a fungus that grows on the faces and wings of bats that are hibernating. As a result, the affected bats wake up excessively and use up their fat reserves, eventually starving to death.

Conservation efforts: It's critical to adhere to best practices when handling and engaging with bats, support conservation efforts that safeguard bat habitats, and support healthy bat populations in order to conserve bat populations and stop the transmission of diseases carried by bats.

Despite the fact that bats may harbor diseases that can be passed on to people and other animals, the risk of transmission is generally low, and the majority of bat populations do not directly endanger human health. Maintaining biodiversity and halting the spread of illness require protecting bat populations and fostering healthy bat habitats.

Lifespan

The longevity of bats varies depending on the species, however most bats live longer than other small animals. On general, bats live longer than other mammals of a similar size, and some species are capable of living in the wild for over 30 years. The lifespan of bats can be summarized as follows:

Lifespan: Bats have a wide range of life spans, with some species only living a few years and others living for many decades. Little insectivorous bats, for instance, may only live for a year or two, whereas larger fruit-eating bats may live for 30 years or longer.

Factors influencing lifetime: Genetics, diet, environment, and reproductive methods are only a few of the variables that determine a bat's lifespan. Due to their specialized diets, some bat species, such as fruit-eating bats that consume high levels of antioxidants, have evolved longer lifespans.

Records for lifespan: A Brandt's bat survived for nearly 41 years to be the oldest known wild bat, while a bigger mouse-eared bat lived for over 33 years to be the oldest known bat in captivity.

The extended lifespans of bats are significant because of their contribution to the preservation of thriving ecosystems. Because of their longer lifespans, bats may perform important tasks including pollination, seed dissemination, and insect control for extended periods of time.

The average lifespan of bats varies depending on the species, however most bats live longer than most other small animals. Bats' extended lifespans are crucial for their function in preserving thriving ecosystems and providing crucial ecosystem services.

Conclusion

In conclusion, bats are intriguing animals with a variety of distinctive traits. They are crucial pollinators, seed dispersers, and pest controls in ecosystems. Most bats do not directly endanger human health, despite the fact that they can harbor diseases that can be spread to humans and other animals. Researchers who are studying the immune system of bats are also very interested in their longevity and capacity to survive in the midst of numerous viruses and other infections. Maintaining biodiversity and halting the spread of illness require protecting bat populations and fostering healthy bat habitats. Ultimately, we can learn a lot from studying and safeguarding bats because they are a significant and fascinating aspect of the natural world.

Thank you